A War-time Journal,
Germany 1914
and German Travel Notes

Harriet Julia Jephson

Contents

A WAR-TIME JOURNAL, GERMANY 1914 AND GERMAN TRAVEL NOTES

BY

Harriet Julia Jephson

PREFACE

refaces are rarely read, yet I have the hardihood to venture on this one because there are certain things in connection with my journal which it is necessary to explain. On returning from Germany, although urged by my friends to publish the story of my experiences, I refused, fearing to do anything which in the smallest degree might prejudice the case of those still in captivity. There came a day, nevertheless, when I read that all English people had left "Altheim." The papers announced that men under forty-five had been interned at Ruhleben, and those over that age had been sent to Giessen. There seemed, therefore, no possible object in further withholding the journal, since, after all, there was nothing in it which could by any possibility affect the fate of others less fortunate than I. Accordingly I sent my manuscript to the *Evening Standard*, which accepted it, and published the first couple of pages. Then, in deference to the wishes of people whose relations were still at "Altheim" (having been sent back from Giessen), I stopped my diary. However, in view of the daily revelations in the Press as regards prisoners in Germany, I have come, after seven months, to the conclusion that nothing I can say will in any degree make the condition of prisoners there worse. Meanwhile it is of supreme interest to compare the opinions and conduct of Germans at the beginning of the war with what they express and observe now. My journal is simply a record made each day of my detention, and although it has no pretension to being literature, it is at least a truthful picture of the state of things as we in Altheim saw them at the beginning of the war. For obvious reasons the place of detention has been given a fictitious name.

HARRIET J. JEPHSON.

A WAR-TIME JOURNAL:
GERMANY, 1914

VILLA BUCHHOLZ, ALTHEIM, *August 1st.*--Last night a herald went round the town and roused everyone, blowing his trumpet and crying, "Kommen Sie heraus! Kommen Sie alle fort!" This was a call to the reservists, all of whom are leaving Altheim. To-day the crowd cheered madly, sang "Heil Dir im Sieger Kranz," and "Deutschland ueber alles," showing the utmost enthusiasm. To my horror, I find that the banks here refuse foreign cheques, and will have nothing to do with letters of credit. I have very little ready money with me, and the situation is not a pleasant one!

August 2nd.--Germany has declared war against Russia! All men old enough to serve are leaving to join the army. Proclamations are posted up in the Park Strasse, and crowds are standing in tense anxiety in groups, discussing matters with grave faces. We don't know how to get away, since all trains are to be used only for the troops while "mobilmachung" is going on. People have got as far as the frontier and been turned back there, and some who left Altheim yesterday are still at Frankfort. I tried to buy an English paper in the town, and was told that none were to be had until England had made up her mind what she was going to do! We think of motorcars to the frontier, or the Rhine boat.

August 3rd.--Alas! all steamers on the Rhine are stopped and motor-cars are impossible, because an order has come out that petroleum is to be reserved for the Government. I made another attempt to cash a cheque to-day, and again the bank refused. A Russian who stood beside me was desperate. He spoke execrable French, and cried excitedly: "Comment donc! je ne puis pas quitter le pays et j'ai une famille et trois femmes!" Poor Bluebeard! his "trois femmes" (wife and daughters) looked terrified and miserable. Our position is incredible and most serious. Still, one cannot but admire the glorious spirit of sacrifice and patriotism which animates all classes of the German people. Just what it was in the war of 1813, when women even cut off their hair and sold it to help their country.

August 4th.--Troops are marching through the streets and leaving for the Front all day long. The ladies of Altheim go to the station as the trains pass through, and give the soldiers coffee, chocolate, cigars, and zwiebacks. They get much gratitude, and the men say (poor deluded mortals): "Wir kriegen fuer Sie" (We fight for you). I saw poor Frau G---- (my doctor's wife) to-day. She was quite calm, but looked miserable. Her eldest son, Dr. T----, left for the front this morning. I sympathised, and she said, choking back a sob: "Man gibt das beste fuer das Vaterland" (one gives one's best for the Fatherland). No letters come, nor papers; and we are only allowed to send postcards written in German.

August 5th.--Our baker has gone to the war, and Dr. G---- 's butler; the schools have shut up, so many masters having been called upon to fight. Even learned professors turn soldiers in this country, and most of the weedy cabhorses here have left Altheim to serve their "Fatherland." My Bade-Frau's husband has gone to the front, and so has our Apotheke; there are no porters left at the station, and a jeweller is doing duty as station-master! The Red Cross Society meet daily, and make preparations for the care of wounded men. Hospitals, private houses, and doctors' houses are getting ready, and all motors have been put at the State's disposal. Insane hatred against Russia exists, and the Russians here are not enjoying themselves! My position is most serious: no money, and no return ticket!

August 6th.--I went out early in quest of news, and looked in at K---- and L----'s. A young clerk, pale with excitement and anger, in reply to my question: "Gibt es etwas neues?" literally hissed at me: "England hat Krieg erklaert" (England has declared war). It was an awful moment, although one was prepared for it in a measure, feeling sure that England would be faithful to her bond.

Next came the Press announcements, "Das unglaubliche ist Tatsache geworden" (The unbelievable is become an accomplished fact). "England, who poses as the guardian of morality and all the virtues, sides with Russia and assassins!" Abuse of Sir Edward Grey, of our Government, and of all things English, follows. When vituperation fails, the "Frankfurter Zeitung" reminds its readers that, after all, such conduct is only what may be expected from "Die historische Perfide Albions." That it is a blow none the less is shown by more than one newspaper beginning "Das Schlimmste ist geschehen." (The worst has happened.) Miss M----, Miss H----, and I went to the "Prince of Wales's Hotel" to see Mr. S----, who had made out a list of the English in Altheim, and tried to telephone to our Consul in Frankfort to ask what he was going to do for our rescue. The telephone people refused to send the message because we were English! Mr. S---- and other men here are doing all they can to secure a train when the mobilisation is over. He advised us to pack up and be ready to start, also not to show ourselves out of doors much, as there is the greatest fury and indignation at present against the English, and to be careful what we said and did. We are all terribly anxious, and it is rather trying for me, as I am the only woman in the place quite alone.

August 7th.--Still no help! Innumerable wild rumours are flying about. They say that those who left Altheim have all come back, unable to get farther than Frankfort. We are beginning to feel hopeless. Nothing about England is in the German papers, and, of course, we see no others. It is quite terrible being without news. Last night there was great scrubbing and scraping of Altheim shop windows, and all the notices: "English spoken here" have disappeared.

There is a mania about spies in Frankfort, we hear, and some Americans yesterday were very roughly handled because their motor bore a French maker's name. The Americans have returned to Altheim, and their motor has been taken to fight for the Fatherland! Our situation is dreadful, but we are keeping up brave hearts. Every day a fresh "Bekanntmachung" (notice) appears; that of to-day was addressed to the children and called upon them to gather in the harvest, the workers having gone as soldiers and turned their "pruning hooks" into swords. My postcards written in German have all come back. One cannot communicate with anyone outside Altheim. What a position! God in His mercy help us! It seems so strange to see German troops marching to the tune of "God Save the King," yet it is Germany's National Anthem too, and these are the words they sing to it:--

"Heil Dir im Sieger Kranz,
Herrscher des Vaterlands,
Heil Kaiser Dir!" etc.

A "Warnung" has now been affixed to trees in the Avenue forbidding Russians, English, French or Belgians to go within 100 metres of the station. The Russians are being hardly used, but so far Germans are quite nice to us. Mrs. N---- tells me a gruesome tale of a Russian lady who left her hotel for Russia smiling, well dressed, and happy. At Giessen all Russians were turned out of the train and put into a waiting-room, and locked up there without any convenience of food, drink, or beds for the night. The following morning they were told to come out and soldiers marched them several miles into the country to a farm-house. Some of the poor creatures were faint from want of food, and others had heart disease, and fell exhausted in the road, the soldiers prodding them with their bayonets to make them get up! After several hours' detention there, they were brought back to Altheim, where the poor lady arrived a pitiable wreck! What an experience! I have been packed up for days!

August 8th.--I went into the Park Strasse this morning to buy a "Frankfurter Zeitung." Outside the shop where I bought it some American women stood gazing at a map of the war, and one said: "I am **disgusted** with England, just disgusted. So degrading of her to help a country like Russia, and side with assassins, just degrading! All we Americans despise her now." I thought to myself: "If I go to prison for it, I will not allow anyone to call my country 'degraded and disgusting.'" So I said, trembling with wrath, "There is nothing 'degrading' in being honourable, nor despicable in keeping true to your word. England promised to protect Belgium's frontier, and she is bound to do it."

Several Germans were gathered round the map, and they scowled at me until I faced them calmly and said: "Jeder man fuer sein Land" (Every man for his country), and they answered quite civilly: "Gewiss!" (Certainly). The Americans in Altheim, I found afterwards, were chiefly of German extraction, which accounted for the woman's behaviour.

Early this morning three men arrived to search my room for weapons. I was in bed, but they pushed past the maid Kaethchen, forced their way in, pried into every corner, and departed. Emile the housemaid here has **four** brothers at the war. Dreadful rumours are flying about as to our destination. One day we hear we are to go to Denmark, another to Holland. Sometimes we are told that we shall not be allowed to leave Germany until the war is over; again that we shall be sent away at a moment's notice; that we shall be left at the frontier, and have to walk for six hours, and carry our own luggage, etc.

The German papers are perfectly horrible in their violent abuse of England, and we are so miserably anxious, not about ourselves, but about our dear, dear country, and how she is faring. Kaethchen said this morning, "Die deutschen in Ausland sind sehr schlecht behandelt" (Germans abroad are very badly treated). "See how well the foreigners are treated *here*," by way of impressing upon me how thankful I ought to be for my mercies.

August 9th.--No papers! No news! No letters! No money! All of us are more or less packed up ready to start. We are warned that no heavy luggage can go with us, and are limited to two small "hand Gepaeck," which we can carry ourselves. I have presented my best hats to Kaethchen, and it consoles me to think how comical she will look under them!--but "flying canvas" is the order of the day.

August 10th.--The "Frankfurter Zeitung" calls England "ehrlos" (dishonour-able), and the Belgian frontier question "only an excuse," and even kind, good Dr. G---- raged against England. One is sick with longing to hear how the war gets on from the English point of view. The papers here never allude to England's move-ments--only to her moral delinquencies. I am so poverty-stricken now I wash my own pocket-handkerchiefs, guimpes, and blouses!

The American part of our community have quite recovered their spirits since money has come for them. The United States is making every effort to rescue her people, and get them back in safety to America. No one seems to concern them-selves about us, and we can't get away while mobilising is going on. All Germans show the greatest deference to Americans, and call them "our honoured guests." We, of course, are the *dis*honoured ones, and in disgrace!

Altheim people so far are passably civil to us, but sometimes one has a dis-agreeable person to deal with, as I had to-day at the Bad Haus. The girl who stamps our tickets refused to pass mine until I could show her my Kur Karte. I had none, and told her so, and asked her why I should pay twenty marks for a card, when I could not get any of the privileges to which it entitled me: the band, terrace, reading-room, and so on. Her answer was a persistent dogged reiteration of "Sie muessen eine Kur Karte haben, sonst koennen Sie nicht baden," and not having twenty marks in the world at present I had to come away without my bath. Every day there are fresh appeals to the patriotism of the people. They are pasted on walls, windows, and even trees.

August 12th.--Such an amusing thing has happened. Mr. S---- said to Dr. ----, "We English have captured your Kronprinzessin Cecilie," without saying that he meant the *ship*, and not the *lady*. As the Government keeps all such disagreeable intelligence dark, it was news to the doctor, and he stoutly contradicted it, and went round the town afterwards telling people: "Just think what liars the English are; they say they have captured our Crown Princess!" We learnt of this prize-taking from the "Corriere della Sera."

August 13th.--The newspapers are full of German victories and abuse of England. Also they declare that the most terrible atrocities have taken place in Belgium, where women have despatched wounded Germans on the field and shot doctors. The indignation is tremendous.

August 14th.--Permission has at last been given for "Fremden" (foreigners) to depart, and also the threats and restrictions as to the railway station have been removed, but we must submit our passports to the police, who send them to Berlin to be stamped by the military authorities, and in about a week we shall be free. "Gott sei Dank!"

August 15th.--I went to the Polizei-Amt, a dreary little house, and found both yard and staircase crammed with people. After waiting a long time in the *queue* I had to beat a retreat, the neighbourhood of Polish Jews being too overpowering! In the afternoon I ventured again with the same result. They say Holland is crammed with refugees, and the hotels so full that people are sleeping on billiard tables even. We are allowed to choose between Switzerland and Holland.

German papers express deepest disappointment that Italy has not been "ehrlich" (honourable) to her "Dreibund," and yet (extraordinary people) the Germans blame us for being true to ours.

August 16th.--I sent a telegram off to Ems this morning, of course written in German, but the official behind the little window where I handed it in refused to send it until I showed him my passport. As I have not yet succeeded in getting through the crowds at the police station I still had mine. We hear dreadful tales of hardships endured by those who have managed to get away from other places. Some went by the Rhine steamers, which are now running, but wherever they passed a fortress they were made to go below. As the cabins were not enough for all, preference was given to other nationalities, and English people had to sit up all night on deck, even in pouring rain. The entire absence of news is for us quite terrible. One feels so out of the world, not knowing what is happening outside our prison doors. The "Frankfurter Zeitung" is full of nothing but boasts and untruths. A fresh "Bekanntmachung" has been posted up forbidding us to leave the town, and ordering us to be indoors by nine o'clock.

August 17th.--The Landsturm has been called out and leaves to-day for the Front. These men are the last to be requisitioned, being elderly.[1] After long waiting among Jews, Infidels, and Turks, I at last got entrance to the Chief of Police's office, had my passport taken, paid one mark fifty, and was told to come back on Thursday, when it would be returned from Berlin. The Chief was a gruff, disagreeable old man, who, to my amiable "Guten Tag" and "Adieu" vouchsafed no reply.

August 18th.--A dreadful blow! We English are forbidden to go to Holland, and told that our destination is to be Denmark. Imagine crossing that mined sea now! For reasons of their own German authorities will not allow any of us to go by or near the Rhine.

August 19th.--The German Press is to me a revelation of bombast, self-righteousness, falsehood, and hypocrisy. What shocks one most is the familiar and perpetual calling upon God to witness that He alone has led the Germans to victory and blessed their cause. I read a poem yesterday, which began "Du Gott der Deutschen," as if indeed the Deity were the especial property of the German Nation! Massacre, pillage, destruction, violation of territory, everything wicked God is supposed to bless! What hideously distorted minds, and where is the sane, if prosaic Teuton of one's imaginings! I wake often in the morning and wonder if all that has happened here has not been a horrible nightmare--if it can be possible in the twentieth century that I, a woman, am a prisoner, and for no sin that one has committed. I cannot order an Einspaenner and drive to the station without a challenge and danger. I cannot possibly get away without my passport. If I attempted to drive to the Rhine my fate might be that of the poor Russians who were shot the other day. In any case I could not leave Germany without my passport nor enter Dutch territory without permission from the Netherlands Consul at Frankfort. It seems all hopeless

---

1   This we were told at the time.

and heartbreaking.

August 20th.--Another terrific blow! Fraulein S---- came into my room this morning and said: "Kein Englaender, kein Auslaender, kann Deutschland verlassen" (no Englishman, no foreigner can leave Germany). I rushed off immediately to the Polizei Amt and found it only too terribly true. Worse! Mr. W---- and Mr. S----, who tried to arrange for a steamer on the Rhine to take us away, have been arrested, and are being tried on a trumped-up charge of *forgery*, and the Company who were the go-betweens demand 3,000 marks because the boat came a certain distance down the river in order to embark us.

(Later) The Englishmen have been acquitted of forgery, but we fear we shall have to pay the L120. I have one mark left!

There is jubilation all over the town as the Germans have taken Belfort. Kaethchen enters triumphantly. "Unter Fuehrung des Kronprinzen von Bayern haben Truppen gestern in Schlachten zwischen Metz und den Vogesen noch einen Sieg erkaempft," and she goes on with the weary old story of "viele tausend Gefangene" (many thousand prisoners).

August 21st.--I found that charming old American friends of mine, the W----s, were here, and I went to see them at the Grand Hotel. They have been to a Nach Kur in Thuringia, and have had most alarming and unpleasant adventures coming back. However, being American their pains and penalties are nearly over. A special train is to take them and their compatriots to the Hague on Wednesday next. They go to the flesh-pots of Egypt, and we are left to eat manna in the wilderness! They can drive in the country, while we poor Britishers may not go outside the town, and oh! how sick we are of the avenues and streets of the red-roofed Bath Houses and shop windows whose contents we know by heart. Mr. W---- told me a good tale of the *chef* of a Hotel here, who was obliged to obey his country's call and join the French forces. When he found German bullets whizzing about him at Muelhausen, he said to himself (so the story goes), "What is my duty? Is it best for me to let these cursed Germans make an end of me, or live to cook another day for my country?" He decided that living was his game, threw his rifle away, lay flat on his face, and let the bullets whistle over him. He was taken prisoner to his great relief, and now lies in Frankfort prison where his German brother chef has visited him! The French of course are a brave nation, but I daresay the poor cook was more at home with his pots and pans than with bayonets and rifles!

No papers! no letters! no news! no chance of escape! Two men were put in prison yesterday for laughing at Germany. Two Russians were stopped in a motor car, and when arms were found upon them they were put up against a wall and shot.

August 22nd.--Altheim has gone mad with joy over the victory near Metz. Church bells chime and German children sing "Deutschland ueber Alles" *ad nauseam*; and the Kur Haus and all private dwellings are draped with bunting. Red Cross people are busy preparing for the wounded--sewing classes are held every day in Bad Haus 8, and the doctors are full of work. Mr. S----, a young Englishman, formerly in the army, has been arrested, and also the hall-porter of the "Grand," and two English valets.

August 24th.--A terrible day! First of all Kaethchen announced with complacency and obvious triumph, that there had been a great victory "ganz herrlich!" and that an English Cavalry Brigade had been cut to pieces at Luneville, and that those who were not killed had "run away"! Of course I did not believe this, but it made one terribly anxious. Then in came Miss H---- saying that two men of our little colony had been arrested and taken to the police-station, whence after examination they were to be sent to Frankfurt. At the Polizei Amt the Officials exhibited the results of their *Kultur* by being rude and rough to the unfortunate people arrested. A Polish woman whose son had been made prisoner sobbed and cried, whereupon the grim old inspector came into the room and said sternly: "Kein Frauen Jammer hier!" ordering her out of the room. I was in the Park Strasse and heard some Germans chuckling and saying: "Zwei Englaender sind verhaftet" (two Englishmen are arrested), looked round, and saw two of our little community, both service men, following each other in Einspaenners, each surrounded by soldiers and fixed bayonets. It was anything but a pleasing sight to me!

August 25th.--The clouds are lifting, thank God! Cheering news has come that we are to be allowed to leave this delightful country in eight days' time; most likely we shall have to travel either by way of Switzerland or Denmark. Those sagacious personages in Berlin seem to imagine that the secrets of the Rhine fortresses will reveal themselves to us as we go by! What a compliment to our powers of clairvoyance!

Fraulein G---- has just been in to see me. Usually she is a most pleasant, gentle little woman, kind and charming; now she is full of scorn and hatred of England. She says the Englishmen were arrested because they were heard to say that German papers were "full of lies." "So they are," said I, "and you can go now and get me arrested too." "Oh, no," said she, "I would not tell on *you*!" In spite of her magnanimity I cannot think our interview was a success. We argued until I said, "If we are to remain friends, we must not discuss the war. I *can*not think England wrong, and as a loyal German you think Germany right. Don't let us talk about it any more."

The "Frankfurter Zeitung" declares that no workmen in England will fight for their country, only the "mercenaries" who are well paid to risk their lives. Oh, this life is hard to bear! Such intense, frightful hatred speaks in every look, in every action of our enemies. It is consoling to remember that their own Nietzsche says: "One does not hate as long as one dis-esteems, and only when one esteems an equal or superior."

August 26th.--A chauffeur at the Bellevue was arrested to-day and taken to Frankfort. He is only twenty, a Glasgow lad, and absolutely harmless.

I am so sick of "Heil Dir im Sieger Kranz" that as the children pass my villa shouting it or "Was ist des Deutschen Vaterland?" I go out on my balcony and retaliate by singing "Rule Britannia." Small children with flags and paper cocked hats, toy swords and tiny drums march through the streets, day after day, singing patriotic songs, whilst (poor dears!) their fathers are being slaughtered in thousands. No reverses are ever reported in the German papers, nothing but victories appear, and Germans are treated like children. If it were not for the "Corriere della Sera" we should be tempted to believe the Allies in a bad way. The "beehrte gaeste" departed this morning. At the station a band played, flags were waved, and every American man and woman was presented with a small white book which contained the telegrams which passed between the belligerent nations at the beginning of the war. Again we hear that Copenhagen is to be our destination.

August 27th.--I saw Dr. G---- this morning. He begged me to be most careful what I said. Two patients of his (English) Levantines were talking on the Terrace, and one said to the other, "We had better shave off our moustaches, or we shall be taken for military men." They were promptly arrested, having been overheard by a spy. We are now ordered to get health certificates, which are to go to Frankfort, and be forwarded to the military authorities in Berlin. There is an idea that we may go away on Tuesday next. We have found out that our passports never went to Berlin at all, but are lying at this moment in the drawer of that old demon in the "Polizei-Amt."

August 28th.--Nothing new. The German papers, as usual, full of their victories and their piety, and their patriotism, and their "Kultur," and goodness knows what not besides. Both Kaisers praising each other and distributing iron crosses *ad lib.*, early though it be in the day. No mention of English troops or England, except to abuse the "Verfluechte" English.

A train of wounded men arrived yesterday, and bandaged and lame soldiers are to be seen limping about the town, looking ghastly pale and ill. At the Lazarett behind the "Prince of Wales' Hotel" there are many sad cases. The Red Cross Society has made every provision for their comfort and happiness possible. Sheets have been hemmed, pillow cases sewn, bandages got ready. The Germans, however, are chary of admitting English women to share their labours, and those who go and offer to help meet with a very chilly reception.

August 29th.--An account has come of the battle of St. Quentin. The "Frankfurter Zeitung" calls it "decisive," and says that the German army has cut off the English army from its base.

August 30th.--Joy at last! Even the "Frankfurter Zeitung" acknowledges that there has been a fight in the North Sea, and that we have sunk German ships, but, of course, it was "overpowering numbers and larger ships" that did it, and the Germans covered themselves with glory as usual. I came home and hung out my flag, the best I could do, a red silk dressing jacket, lined with white, and draped over a blue silk parasol, which I tied knob out, to look like a pole.

On our church door to-day was posted a typewritten notice: "We have smashed your army on the French Continent,(!) and we will smash *you too* if you dare to ring your bell!"

August 31st.--I heard a small boy singing to-day:

"Wo liegt Paris, Paris liegt Hier,
Den fingen drauf' Das nehmen Wir."

I pray it may not prove prophetic, but they all talk of occupying Paris as a certainty, and the German Emperor has invited a number of his Generals to dine with him there on the 12th of September. I hear that a doctor went into the Prince of Wales' Hotel to-day, and saw stuck up in the hall the words: "Das Seegefecht in der Nordsee" (in which of course we were victorious). He tore it down and stamped on it. An altruistic German waiter thinking to please the English guests had put the first sheet of the "Frankfurter Zeitung" in a prominent position to console them for the many defeats we are supposed to have had. John Burns' speech at the Albert Hall is reported in full in the German newspapers, headed "Eine Rede des ehemaligen Englischen Minister, John Burns. England gegen seine wahren interessen" (a speech of the former English minister,[2] John Burns. England against her true interests). No passports yet! No release! This suspense is wearing!

September 1st.--The sentimentality of the Germans is amazing! They cannot even insert a simple notice of a death on the battlefield without this sickly parade, "Heute starb den Heldentod furs Vaterland, unser innigste-geliebter einziger Sohn," etc. Always a "hero's death" and "for his Fatherland." A fresh "Bekanntmachung" has appeared, we prisoners of war are not to leave the town, not to stand in groups ("rotten" they call it) talking in the streets, to be in our houses at 9 p.m., etc. Two ex-Frankfort prisoners have been sent for by the Chief of the Police accused of indiscreet talking. "I hear," said the great man, "you say you were fed on nothing but bread and water in prison." "No," said Mr. ----, "I had soup in the middle of the day, and coffee and bread at night, and in the morning." "Then why do you tell lies!" Such utter childishness, to believe every scrap of unkind gossip!

September 2nd.--We are buoyed up with hope, as they talk of our getting away this week! It *will* be delightful to leave this perpetual bell-ringing and flag-waving and Vaterlandslieder behind us!

September 3rd.--The whole of Altheim went mad last night, processions, bands, marchings all night, and such a noise that at last a nurse had to come out from the Lazarett near the Park and beg the revellers to think of the poor wounded sick, and spare them. No one could sleep! The last blow has come, our church is closed!

September 4th.--Despair! The American Ambassador at Berlin has telegraphed that we English are not to leave! The Russians are going, but our treatment is retaliatory, because they say England is detaining German women, and Russia lets them

---

2   This speech I have since learnt was an absolute invention.

go. To make all worse Fraulein S----, tired of keeping me so long for nothing, has given me notice to quit at the moment when for three days I have had no greater fortune than 2d. in my pocket. Where I am to go, or who will take me in without money I can't imagine! The American Ambassador in Berlin and Mr. Ives, the American Vice-Consul at Frankfort, are working untiringly and most kindly for us. We do not complain of actual harsh treatment, although to be turned adrift in the world without money by one whose tenant I had been for five years is hardly kind. However, war is war undoubtedly. Mr. Ives is from the Southern States, Mr. H----, his Chief, from the Northern. The Scotch chauffeur has been released after a week in prison. He looks pale and dispirited, "a sadder," and no doubt "a wiser man."

September 5th.--The "Times" of the 5th August has turned up in Altheim. It has gone the round of our little community until such a worn, creased remnant reached me, that I had much ado to keep it together until I could master its contents. One felt a second Rip Van Winkle, awaking after a long sleep, our world being so confined here. At last I have discovered how to get money from England. One writes to the American Embassy in Berlin, and encloses a telegram (with postal order for the same) to one's banker in London, instructing him to pay the sum of money wanted to the American Embassy in London, to be forwarded through their kind offices to the Embassy in Berlin. The telegram to be written on a sheet of foolscap paper, with the full name and address of the sender, and the name also of the nearest American Consul. No letters can be sent through this channel.

September 6th.--No church now! Even that taken from us! The American Vice-Consul has been here, and still thinks that we may get away in a fortnight. We are sick with hoping and being disappointed. The German Press full of the most virulent abuse of England, "treacherous," "hypocritical," "lying," "cowardly," "boastful," there is no bad name they don't call her! Russia and France and Belgium get no lashings of scorn and fury and hatred such as England does! At last the account of Sir Edward Goschen's interviews with Von Jagow and Bethmann Hollweg has appeared in the German papers. I had read it all in the "Corriere della Sera" long ago. They talk of stopping Italian papers in Germany since they are pro-English (in German, "lying").

Most of my English friends here went to the German church to-day. The Pfarrer pointed out to his congregation how clearly God had favoured their cause, how victory had followed victory, the virtuous, religious people triumphing over the wicked, ungodly nations. Then he spoke of the day so near when Germany should annihilate the "Macht von England," and teach her when crushed and humbled "die Wahrheit," Religion and Morality! Humph!

September 7th.--Wonder of wonders! no bell-ringing to-day, nor processions of singing youngsters, so we hope there is a lull in the "Sieges."

Miss H---- went last week to have her hair washed, and during the process her hair-dresser remarked casually to her, "We shall be in Paris in a day or two, and in London in another week, and when we have conquered England as well as France you will all have to learn to speak German." This shows the amazing conceit and arrogance of the people. Poor, ignorant things, they are quite hoodwinked by their rulers--and even look forward to seeing their Kaiser "Emperor of Europe"! One day we read that a bag has been made of 30,000 Russians, the next that the number was understated, and that it is 70,000. As for Belgians and French, every day 10,000 men and guns *ad lib.* are captured, and the poor silly people believe it all. Villas and streets are still beflagged, and by this time we know every patriotic song in the "Vaterlandslieder" book by heart. One tries to be plucky, but our hearts are very sad just now.

Paris seems doomed, and apparently the French have abandoned hope too, since Poincare and his Cabinet have gone to Bordeaux. The German Press call him a "Feiger" (Coward).

September 9th.--Unaccountably the forward march seems to have been checked, although we don't know why. Maubeuge has fallen, and of course the usual bell-ringing and bunting and singing has celebrated the victory. We cannot understand what our troops are doing. There is no mention of them in the German papers, only columns of sneers and abuse of England.

September 10th.--A rumour has reached us that the Crown Prince has been captured, and that the enemy is retreating. No official confirmation has come to hand however; but the flags are down at last, and the jangling of bells has ceased, and we have not heard "Deutschland ueber Alles" for twenty-four hours, "Gott sei Dank"! Prince Joachim is wounded, and he has sent a telegram worded after the manner of his dear Papa, thanking God who in His goodness permitted him to be wounded for his beloved Fatherland. I wonder what Frederick the Great would have thought of these boastful warriors. We English are looked upon with horror as the brutal barbarians who use dum dum bullets, and Sir Edward Grey's dignified disclaimer is reported under the polite heading "Grey leugnet" (Grey lies).

September 11th.--Nothing new in the situation, but we rejoice to see grave faces and groups looking solemn in the streets, and talking in subdued voices, and thank God! we hear no bell-ringing! Everything cheering we read in the "Corriere della Sera" is denied in the "Frankfurter Zeitung" or given as a production of the "Luegen Fabrik" (manufactory of lies).

September 12th.--The Germans seem depressed, no flags, no bands, and although there is a notice posted up in the town to say that the Crown Prince has achieved another victory, there is evidently something unsatisfactory in the background to counterbalance this. I draw deductions from the "Frankfurter Zeitung," which has a bitter article entitled "Torheiten" (Folly), and which speaks of the "Kindische Freudengeheul" (childish howls of joy) of the English and French Press, because "ein parr Kalonnen deutscher Soldaten ein Stuck weges zurueckgezogen haben" (two columns of German soldiers had withdrawn a bit of the way back). Then the writer contrasts the boastful words ("prahlender woerte") of England with the self-restraint and pious calm and virtuous behaviour of Germany. One has only to look at the postcards in the Park Strasse to see which of the combatants is boastful. England is drawn as ignominiously lying on the ground (when she isn't running away) and Germany invariably is kicking or thrashing her.

People are less friendly than at first, though the bath attendants, people in the Inhalatorium, and doctors are most kind. I had tea at Mueller's with Miss H---- the other day. There were at least thirty empty chairs in the tea-room, but a German woman marched up to the chair on which I had laid my daily newspaper, and ordered me to take it off, as she must have my chair! She was stout and ugly, and had a way of doing her hair which, as a writer says, "alone would have proved impeccable virtue in the face of incriminating circumstantial evidence." For all their "Kultur" Germans are gross, and to the last degree inartistic. Their "nouveau art" is repulsive; their dressing outrageously ugly, and their cooking atrocious. I have watched them here year after year tramping up and down the shady walks stolidly drinking, wearing garments of ingeniously devised ugliness and blind to "l'inutile beaute." There is no variety of type nor individuality of person in either men or women. These worthy ***Hausfrauen*** have no grace of dainty frills, diaphanous lace or rustling petticoats. They are obviously and incontestably of the class described by a witty writer to whom "a lace petticoat is as much a badge of infamy as a cigarette on the stage." The German proletariat cannot be susceptible to externals, else the universal sad-coloured skirt, the ill-fitting blouse and the ugly hat worn by his women-folk could not find favour in his eyes.

Life in Altheim has changed under war conditions. The Kur Haus is closed, there are no teas on the Terrace or promenadings to the strains of Grieg or Strauss, or theatrical performances. The German Kur-Gaeste have left, and only the Russian, English and a few Belgian prisoners of war remain. Russians here are chiefly of a very low class. Most of the women go about bareheaded, and all are rough and unkempt and dirty-looking. I fancy some of them have suffered much privation, but happily their order of release has come. They will have to travel by Denmark, Sweden and across to Petrograd. The weather is autumnal, and they have only summer clothes, like us. We cannot help them, having so little money ourselves. I have had to borrow twice, and tried to sell my jewellery without success, but I have developed a latent and unsuspected talent for laundry work. The pretty summer shops in the Park Strasse are now closed, and the sound of beating mattresses is heard everywhere; the blinds of most of the villas are drawn down, and the families having no longer lodgers have descended to their winter quarters on the ground floor. Only a few ***einspaenners*** are left, as both ***Kutschers*** and horses are gone to meet a "Heldentod" for their Fatherland.

One sees white-capped nurses and Red Cross Ambulance men and wounded and bandaged warriors everywhere. When recovered, the soldiers get three days leave to visit their families, and then return to the Front. Poor souls! Shops are chiefly tended by women nowadays, and the German Frau is not a capable shopkeeper like the French woman. A "Drogerie" here is presided over by the wife of the man who owns it, in his absence at the war. She is a gentle, rather pretty creature, but amazingly slow and stupid. If tooth-powder be asked for, she mounts a ladder, searches among a hundred bottles, shakes her head despairingly, and wonders where her "Mann" has put it. Outside her Kueche and house, the German woman does not shine, but she is a faithful unselfish wife, and a good and affectionate mother. Mr. Ives thinks we shall certainly get away next week. I hope so! The weather is cold and rainy, and there is no fire-place in my room.

September 13th.--The Altheim daily papers complain that they are inundated with foolish questions over the telephone. "Ist Namur belgisch oder franzoesisch?" (Is Namur Belgian or French?)

"Gehen die Schottlaender wirklich mit nackten Beinen in die Schlacht?" (Do the Highlanders really go into battle with naked legs?)

"Wie lange wird es ungefaehr dauern, bis die Deutschen Paris eingenommen haben?" (How long will it be before the Germans have taken Paris?) and so on.

September 14th.--Again rumours of our going, but even though release will be most welcome, we all dread the journey. Terrible tales come to us of the treatment meted out to foreigners crossing the frontier. Many English were turned out of Wiesbaden and sent here. At F---- they had their luggage searched, and the ladies of the party were stripped to the skin by women who even combed their hair to see if by any ingenuity they had concealed plans and drawings in the puffs and coils, two soldiers with fixed bayonets mounting guard meanwhile outside. No doubt we shall remember this journey to the end of our lives, but what can you expect from a people whose Prophet Nietzsche says, "What is more harmful than any vice? Pity for the weak and helpless--Christianity!"

September 15th.--The singular absence of humour of the Germans often amuses me. I think it was Palmerston who described Germany as "that land of damned Professors." They are all so desperately in earnest, and their "Kultur" is so serious, that jokes and fun seem like blasphemy. My penury has again been relieved by Mr. S----'s kind loan of L1. Lady M---- came in to tell me that the American Vice-Consul had telegraphed to Mr. W---- the good news that we are all to go on Monday, Tuesday or Wednesday next. I have heard this story so often that I am utterly sceptical. We conclude that things are going badly for the enemy, since there is no bell-ringing, and the flags have been taken in.

September 16th.--I hear that no men who have served in the Army or Navy are to be allowed to go with us. To-day's "Frankfurter Zeitung" thinks that England must be at her last gasp, or she would not have "barbarians such as Indians, Japanese and *Highlanders*" fighting her battles for her! They also declare on "unimpeachable evidence" that India is in a state of revolt, and that the Japanese are to be despatched at once to quell the rebellion. Any misfortune to the British delights them.

September 17th.--The B----s, who to our envy have received special passes to go to Denmark, got as far as Hamburg and then had their passports taken from them. The Chaplain and his wife disappeared one morning, and we learn that he obtained a special pass on the ground of being a clergyman. He was heard to utter something about the "Bishop of London," and perhaps that was the talisman. Lady M---- tells me that they have arrived in Hamburg, we wonder what their fate will be!

A delightful story has just reached me from an Italian source. In the church of a Convent Hospital in France, one of the sisters was praying aloud with immense fervour, and when she came to the "Confiteor" she said: "C'est ma faute! c'est ma faute! c'est ma tres grande faute," whereupon uprose a Turco crying out: "Ah! non! ma Soeur! c'est la faute a Guilleaume!"

September 18th.--A letter at last! but only one from the American Consul at Frankfort, saying that the Foreign Office wanted to know my whereabouts as several friends had inquired about me and my safety. I can't imagine why, when America rescued her stranded citizens long ago, and sent them money to get home, we should be suffering like this. Nothing more about the phantom train! Our nerves are becoming wrought up, and we are developing unexpectedly irritable and argumentative natures. The weather is amazingly windy and horribly cold, one shivers in summer garments, and cannot afford to buy warmer things. A leading article in the "Frankfurter Zeitung" gives us a grain of comfort, since it is headed "Geduld und Zuversicht" (patience and confidence), and begins,

"In consequence of the victorious news of the first weeks, those remaining at home had become accustomed to constant victories, and the pause in the news of the battlefield of the West is a great trial of patience." Long may that trial last! On the whole we ought to be thankful that we are in Hesse and not in Prussia. The Hessians are a simple, kindly people, pleasant, and good tempered. I have known Germany well for eighteen years. When first we travelled in the Fatherland I found each Duchy, or Kingdom, or Principality, devoted to its own particular Ruler, and little outside it mattered to its people. Nowadays there are no Hessians or Wuertembergers, not even Saxons or Bavarians, but all are Germans, and for one photograph of the Grand Duke of Hesse and his Duchess you will see here one hundred of "Unser Kaiser" and "Unsere Kaiserin." They have become Imperialists, and the ambitious spirit which animates them is shown by the act of a soldier at Liege who chalked up on a wall: "Kaiser Wilhelm the Second, Emperor of Europe."

I have now 2d. left in the world, and have not taken my inhalation for two days, not being able to pay for it. The money I telegraphed for has not yet come, and life seems very difficult! I think of the old lines:

> "'Tis a very good world we live in,
> To lend, or to spend, or to give in;
> But to beg, or to borrow, or get a man's own,
> 'Tis the very worst world that ever was known."

September 19th.--At the eleventh hour and when I seemed at the end of my resources, help came from a most unexpected quarter! I can never cease to be grateful for the goodness and kindness which relieved my distress. The Germans look downcast, the Russians jubilant. How paternal this Government is no one who has not lived in Germany can imagine. For instance, above the nearest pillar box I saw a notice written "Don't forget address and stamps!"

September 20th.--Our passports are now in the hands of the military authorities at Frankfort, and Mr. Ives, the American Vice-Consul, is doing all in his power to get us leave to go. The Superintendent of the Inhalatorium is most kind and sympathetic. She inquired why I had not been there for three days, and when I told her "Gar kein Geld" (no money) was the cause, she cried with real feeling, "Schrecklich!" (terrible). Any thing to do with money or the want of it appeals to the Teutonic mind, although the Germans sneer at us for being a nation of shopkeepers. There are two words we hope never to hear again, "Kultur" and "Unser." "Unser Deutschland," "Unser Kaiser," "Unser Kultur." How weary and trite are these! What an extraordinary mixture the Germans are, brave, conceited, sentimental, prosaic, patriotic, and yet no people so soon lose their national characteristics, and become citizens of another country as Germans. Many of their intellectual poses are absolutely morbid. They adore Ibsen as a playwright and despise Goldsmith and Sheridan; they worship Gauguin, and the school of Impressionists, and have little appreciation nowadays for pre-Raphaelitism. They are intensely and truly musical, and it is amazing, taking into consideration their extraordinary lack of humour, that they should be such accomplished students of Shakespeare, but of real wit or humour the

German possesses not an atom. Take, for instance, the modern novels of Suderman, of Rudolph Herzog, of Rudolph Stratz, of Bernard Kellerman, of Paul Heyse, and you will find intense seriousness, tragedy, pathos, masterly drawing of character, and absolutely no fun from cover to cover. As for the "Fliegende Blaetter," the German "Punch," it is the sickliest imitation of humour possible to conceive. Foremost in science, the German is yet a neophyte in the graces and arts of life. What cooking! what clothes!

September 22nd.--If we may believe such good news we are to be released from this irksome life, and set at liberty next Saturday. Our joy is much damped, however, by hearing that none of the men are to be allowed to leave, and, of course, their wives stay with them. Mr. Ives has made a special journey to Berlin on behalf of our poor men, but the authorities are obdurate.

People say that the loss of life in this terrible war is beyond belief as far as the Germans are concerned. To hide this the Emperor requests that no one shall wear mourning for the dead until the war is over. Also, no complete catalogues of casualties are issued, only lists for each kingdom, or duchy, so that the bulk of the people have no idea of the waste of life. The wounded being so numerous, the doctors now have little time to attend to them on the spot, and therefore they are put into trains and sent off to "Lazaretts" sometimes before even their wounds are washed. A Belgian lady who had a special police permit to go to Frankfort, returned this afternoon in a train full of wounded soldiers. One of these was put into her carriage. He had been badly shot in the arm; his sleeve was soaked with blood, and that had coagulated; his wound had never been washed, and French earth was still on his boots, and yet he had been sent in this condition from Rheims to Giessen!

September 23rd.--Terrible news! A telegram was posted up in the town this morning, saying that three English "Panzerkreuzers" had been sunk by one German submarine. Of course the church bells pealed, and the flags came out, and the children sang "Nun danket alle Gott," because 950 brave Englishmen had gone under. We are much depressed, and our depression is aggravated by the want of occupation here. We dare not sketch for fear of being "verhaftet" (arrested). It is no good writing because every scrap of paper will be taken from us on the frontier; nobody I know plays bridge, and so I read and walk all day long. Miss H---- tells me that a rude young clerk in the "Loewen-Apotheke" refused to talk English to her this morning, "You will have to learn German now, because we shall be in London within a fortnight," said he! No German I have yet known foresees any other result of this war but success. The Fatherland Commissariat, according to the Italian papers, leaves much to be desired. The unfortunate soldiers are almost starving, and often live for days together on raw carrots, turnips, herbs, or any other vegetable they can root up out of the ground. The doctors are puzzled because men have died of such seemingly slight wounds. One case seemed so incomprehensible that an autopsy was decided on, and a raw root with fragments of earth upon it was found in the poor creature's stomach. The Russians left at 5 a.m. this morning, men and women. It is more than hard that our poor men should be left behind. Lady M----, who has been ill, and her daughter, an invalid lady, and her maid, were given special passes to go a couple of days ago. Miss M---- and Miss G---- went to the police station armed with these passes, and requested to have their passports back. "The Demon" curtly refused. "But you *must* give them to us," said Miss M----. "Don't say *muessen* to me!" said "the Demon," "bitten is the word!" (Don't say *must* to me, *beg* is the word).

September 24th.--Joyfully packing! A last meeting was held at the "Prince of Wales' Hotel" where kind Mr. S---- presided, and we all received instructions for our journey, and our long detained passports!

Fifty women and children go. We sleep in Frankfort, and cross from Flushing to Folkestone. Oh! that terrible mined sea, and the "untersuchung" of the Frontier. I tremble for this Diary, all letters I have destroyed.

FRANKFORT, *September 25th.*--We are still in the enemy's country of course, but have come out of our prison Altheim. All were early at the Bahn-Hof. There for the last time, please God! we found our old horror the Chief of Police. He had a long paper in his hand, and read out our names; "Hamilton?" "Here!" "Your passport?" (which he scrutinised as if he had never seen such a thing before), and so on. As we got our precious papers back we passed through the barrier, where our tickets were clipped, and on to the platform above. The train when it came in was crammed with soldiers, and we were advised to wait two hours for the next, but (to a woman) we all preferred travelling third, or even fourth class, rather than remain another hour where we had suffered so much. Miss G---- told me afterwards that she had travelled with two German men, who cursed England up and down, using the most horrible language about her.

Presently a wounded soldier came into the carriage, and they asked him where he had been fighting. "On the Western Frontier," said he.

"With the French?"

"Yes."

"Did you see the English?"

"No."

"Of course not! They had all run away. Cowards, cowards!"

These are the things which make life so unendurable in an enemy's land. I was sent here to the "Hessicher-Hof," which, although it masquerades under another name, I had no difficulty in recognising as the former "Englischer-Hof." Miss H---- went to the "Hotel Bristol," and when she got there found over the door the one word "Hotel." What we women should have done without the able committee who arranged all details for us with such kindness and thoroughness, I cannot imagine.

September 28th.--There were few tears shed when we steamed out of Frankfort two days ago on our way to home and freedom. It was wonderful to feel that we might talk above a whisper in the railway-carriage; amazing that we had not to scrutinize carefully every corner to be sure no spies lurked there, and most delightful of all to know that we had got beyond the reach of the Demon of the Burg-Strasse. Egotistically enough we went over in retrospect our anxieties, disappointments and miseries. Should we ever get rid of that evil shadow, we wondered, which had darkened so cruelly two weary months of our lives!

Now and then we looked out of the windows with distaste--agreed that the outskirts of Frankfort were hideous with their obtrusive and insistent collection of factory chimneys; and shuddered at the distant and beautiful background of mountain and forest, to us so teeming with painful memories. We exclaimed at the unsightliness of the huge skeleton lettering proclaiming to all the world that a *maschinen-Fabrik* was below. Even when we entered a bucolic region of modest gardens and saw nothing more aggressive than cabbages and turnips, we turned away from the sight with aversion. Yet the villages are picturesque enough, and so are the towns. Timber-framed and gabled houses, steeply pitched red roofs and stunted grey and mossy church spires, certainly make no unpleasing picture. In happier days I have admired the grape-vines meandering over the whitewashed cottages, and marvelled at the monotony of taste which furnished every window-ledge with exactly four pots of scarlet geraniums. Now, nothing pleased us that was German; scenery, architecture or people! "This," we said to ourselves, is "the sunny Rhineland through which we are passing, and we see no obvious signs as we go by of the struggle which is devastating Belgium and menacing France." At the first station, however, we realised that Germany was indeed at war. Red Cross nurses seemed everywhere. Long tables were spread with snowy cloths and bore coffee urns, zwiebacks, hoernchen and huge bowls of steaming soup ready for the poor wounded as they pass through. Now and then pale bandaged faces looked out at us from passing trains, and men on crutches hobbled by, and the horrors of mutilating war came home to us all. At Goch we had to show our passports, and have our luggage examined, but the reality proved not nearly so bad as our imaginings, and on the whole the officials were kind and courteous compared to our Altheim demon. The sun was setting blood-red behind a distant line of black forest when we left Goch and our enemies and imprisonment behind us and entered the Land of Promise.

We had all been saddened in the morning to learn that Mr. Ives' strenuous efforts to get permission for the men left behind to go soon, had met with a curt refusal from the Commandant at Frankfort. "When England returns our men, not before, and she had better be quick about it," said he. But how true is Rochefoucauld's cynical epigram--"Nous avons tous assez de force pour supporter les maux d'Autrui!" Even our sympathy with, and sorrow for, those left in Altheim could not damp the joy we felt to be free again; and when we quitted Goch, the German frontier station, I thought how blessed would be that day when "They shall beat their swords into ploughshares and their spears into pruning hooks; nation shall not lift up a sword against nation, neither shall they learn war any more. But they shall sit every man under his vine and under his fig-tree; and none shall make them afraid."

GERMAN TRAVEL NOTES
"TAKIN' NOTES"

He who knows his Rhine and loves it must take of its charms in small doses, or satiety is the outcome. There are those, of course, who can travel from Dan to Beersheba and cry, "'Tis all barren"; but the ordinarily intelligent traveller may find much to delight and interest on the banks of the Rhine, always provided that he suits his mood to his environment, and takes but little of Rhine scenery at a time. For surely between Coblentz and Bingen there is an iteration as regards castles and ruins which is downright wearisome. Do we not between these points find Lahneck, Marksburg, Sterrenberg, Liebenstein, The Mouse, Rheinfels, The Cat, Schoenburg, Gutenfels, The Pfalz, Stahleck, Furstenberg, Hohneck, Sooneck, Falkenburg, Rheinstein, and Ehrenfels?

Moreover, there is an affinity of form and colour and, indeed, of situation between all these which produces the effect of perpetual repetition. And we owe Byron a grudge for having written such trite words as "the castled crag" in relation to the Rhine, since no commonplace mind of the present day acquainted with his works but has fallen back on "the castled crag" to describe Drachenfels or Marksburg or Rheinfels, because, forsooth, its own English is too limited to supply a better adjective. So it is that conventional and inadequate English is perpetuated and individual force and expression are lost because people accept the ideas of others and will not seek language to convey their own.

All of which above prosing is the result of a day on the Rhine when the thermometer registered 74 deg. to 84 deg. in the shade, and a white vapour hid the banks of the river from Koeln till close on Bonn. At Bonn a huge party of "personally-conducted" American tourists came on board. Their sharp, keen, eager, shrewd faces and shrill voices proclaimed their nationality at the outset. They were all obviously outside the pale of Society, and their thirst for information and keen interest in their surroundings were amazing. One learned before long that they had "done" the Paris Exhibition and meant to have a "look in" at most European countries before sailing from Naples. They took the whole ship into their confidence before a quarter of an hour had passed; and we shared alike in thrilling intelligences conveyed through the medium of Baedeker's pages. "The castled crag" resounded from one end of the boat to the other; and as for Roland and Hildegunde, the tragedy of their lives was discussed, and exclaimed over, and lamented, until, happily, a bend of the river hid Nonnenwerth from sight.

In emphatic contrast to the nervous alertness of the Yankee was the spectacle of the middle-class German and his ways. He sat by his plain, stout, ill-dressed Frau, with his back to the scenery, and ate. Occasionally he spoke in monosyllables: more often he drank; but the end and object of his Rhine trip seemed to be that of consuming as much food as lay within the limits of possibility. What Nemesis has in store for him and those of his manner of life I can only imagine!

At a table near us sat three women and two men. Directly we left Koeln a waiter set forth trays in front of them laden with coffee, zwiebacks, hoernchens, and eggs. This meal over, they sat sleepily blinking their eyes, whisking away flies, and mopping the moisture from their faces until the sound of "Eis! meine Herrschaften!" "Bier! meine Herrschaften!" roused them from their lethargy. Ices and beer and cherries and peaches successively filled up the weary hours until "the tocsin of the soul, the dinner bell," carried joy to their hearts. I can never forget the rapturous look of anticipation and satisfaction which those stolid middle-class Teutonic countenances wore when "Mittagsessen" was announced. They shook off their normal and habitual torpidity, and cheerfully elbowed their neighbours, nearly tumbling down the companion-ladder in their eagerness to be first in the field. They lost no time over the unlovely detail of tucking a corner of their napkins down their necks, and smoothing its folds over their protuberant persons; and they studied the Speise-Karte with a conscientiousness that was worthy of a better cause.

Dinner began with a tolerably good soup, followed by tough roast beef, cut in thick slices and garnished with carrots, peas and beans. Next came veal, equally uneatable, and then a surprise in the shape of Rhine salmon; after which followed chicken, salad, and *compote*. Finally, a stodgy pudding, sufficiently satisfying, and dessert. Not one item of the menu was neglected by the five. They calmly and conscientiously and readily ate through the Speise-Karte from start to finish. Then they returned to deck, only to order coffee and ices, and called for a bottle of champagne, three of light Rhine wine, and a plateful of peaches; out of which they brewed a cup, ladling it from a Taunus ware bowl into their long Munich glasses, and sipping it lazily all the afternoon between such trifles as Kuchen and fresh relays of cherries. They ate and drank from Koeln to Bingen with rare intervals of dozing, and I never once saw any of the party take the faintest interest in the Rhine, so far as its banks were concerned.

It was a relief to turn from such grossness to its antithesis in the shape of two American ladies who sat near us. They were well-preserved, well-bred spinsters under forty. Everything about them was dainty and exquisitely neat. I likened them in my mind to bowls of dried rose-leaves--the freshness gone, the perfume left. Such was their intense and intelligent interest in travel that, rather than lose a timber-framed village or historic castle, a vineyard or watch-tower, they abstained from lunch and picnicked lightly on deck off tea and eggs and hoernchen. They knew the legends of the Rhine as you and I know (or ought to know) our Prayer-Books. They had studied the history of Germany, and mastered the intricacies alike of the Thirty Years' War and of the Hohenzollern pedigree; and they talked well, expressing their ideas in good Saxon words; at times, perhaps a trifle pedantic, but never offensively so.

As the day wore on the temperature became almost overpowering. The water reflected a blinding glare, and a heat like that of a burning fiery furnace was radiated from the engines. I was wondering whether a hammock in a cool English garden would not have been more desirable, when I heard a plaintive, uneducated American voice behind me ask a question of its mate which exactly embodied my own unuttered sentiments:

"What *I* want to know, Jake, is: Is this pleasure, or ain't it? Did we come here to enjoy ourselves, or what?"

JAKE: "Wall, I guess you ain't used to travelling around, my dear, and you don't understand it. Oh, yes" (with an obvious effort), "this is real fust-class pleasure, this is!"

MRS. JAKE: "Wall, I'm darned! I'd as lief be in our store."

JAKE: "Sakes alive! You *do* surprise me! Think what Keren-Happuch Jones will say when you mention casual on your return something that happened when you was sailing up the Rhine. She'll die of envy, she will, and spite to think you've seen more'n her."

MRS. JAKE (cheered somewhat): "Wall, I reckon, Jake, there's summat in that. Keren-Happuch don't like anyone to do what she don't do."

JAKE: "And then, my dear, think of your noo bonnet from Paris! That'll be another pill for Keren-Happuch to swallow."

MRS. JAKE: "My! Yes! I don't think much of Europe, anyway, but I could never have bought that bonnet in Baltimore. But, Jake, do look on the map and tell me when we get to Heidelberg."

JAKE: "It ain't any good my lookin', my dear, for I wasn't raised to these sort of things, and I'm darned if I know where to find it."

A groan from Mrs. Jake, followed by: "Wall, I reckon when I find myself again in No. 9, Mount Mascal Street, I won't want to go travelling around even to cut out Keren-Happuch Jones."

I came to the rescue at this point, and showed the good lady where Heidelberg lay. She was a hard-featured, plain woman of some thirty-eight summers, her hair was dragged back uncompromisingly from her forehead, and there were no "adulteries of art" about either coiffure or costume.

"You see," she said apologetically, "Jake here and me are travelling around, and the only way we can get on is to ask for a ticket to a place, and never stop travelling till we get there. We speak German all right because my parents were Germans, and Jake was born in Germany; but he don't know much about it because he was only two years old when he left it eight-and-thirty years ago. We thought we'd like to see the Paris Exposition, but my! it ain't to be compared to the Chicago Exhibition, and as for Paris, it can't come up to Noo York, and these river steamers ain't a patch on the Hudson River boats, and I don't think much of Europe anyway."

Jake, a good-looking, gentle-mannered man, tried to soften the asperity of his wife's strictures without success. He evidently adored her.

"The way we travel," resumed Mrs. Jake, "is to think of a place we've heard of, and to ask for a ticket to it. Now, we'd heard of Paris and Cologne, and Heidelberg, and Baden, and Dresden, and Berlin, and Hamburg, but we don't know now how they come--see? So we hev' to go cavortin' around to find out which to take next. A gentleman way back at Cologne"--she pronounced it "Klon"--"told me Heidelberg came next. I quite thought Baden was near Hamburg, and that we should take it last; but they tell me it ain't, and that, you see, has upset all our calculations. Guess you're a Londoner, anyway; thought so by your accent!"

When we left the steamer at Bingen, the last I heard of Mrs. Jake was a plaintive moan:

"Guess I don't think much of Europe, anyway, and I wouldn't come again, not even to cut out Keren-Happuch!"

OF SOME FELLOW TRAVELLERS AND
THE CATHEDRAL OF MAINZ.

Ja Wohl! Frau Rittergutsbesitzer. I have lived in the Herr Professor's house for five-and-thirty years. I have pickled his cabbage and preserved his fruit. I have minced with my own hand the pork for his sausages before they had mincing-machines in Schleswig-Holstein. I have seen personally to the smoking of his hams and fish. I make his Apfelkuchen and Nusskuchen myself, and do not buy them in the shop, like that lazy Hausfrau opposite us at No 2, who comes from that God-forgotten country England, where all the women are so badly brought up. I grant you that what I do is no more than the duty of every God-fearing German *Haushaelterin*; none the less, I do not mean all my work to go for nothing, and I will not be ousted by a hussy! In the time of the *vielbedauerten* mother (Frau Regierungsrat Lenbach) I had no worries about his matrimonial affairs; she looked after those. But *sieh mal*, Frau Riedel, now the care of him is on my shoulders. He has no more idea of taking care of himself than a baby! He is exactly like that learned man--I think it was our great Neander--who was running out of his college one day and ran into a cow; so he pulled off his hat and said, 'Gnaedige Frau, ich bitte um Verzeihung' ('Gracious lady, I beg your pardon'), and went on; and the week after he came tearing round the same corner, thinking, I suppose, of those heathen gods and goddesses whose pictures shame a modest woman to look at, and he ran up against a lady, so he cried out: 'Oh! du dumme Kuh! warum kommst du mir immer in den Weg?' ('Oh, you stupid cow, why will you always get in my way?') Yes, my Herr Professor is just like that--quite as stupid, though they call him so wise and clever; and what chance has a born innocent like he is against a designing spinster of forty-five who makes him presents of *Weihnachtstollen* at

Christmas, ***Oster-Eier*** at Easter, and ***Geburtstagstorte*** on his birthday? I ask you what chance of escape a poor ***Junggeselle*** has?

"Told him she wanted to marry him! Not I. Why, ***liebe Frau***, I have not lived sixty-five and a half years in this world for nothing! If I let him suppose she was in love with him, that would be the very way to make him like her. So as I laid the cloth for the Herr Professor's ***Abendtisch***, I remarked casually that Fraeulein Bettine Meyer was not at all a bad sort of woman really, and that she had some excellent qualities, if only she did not make herself so ridiculous. 'How ridiculous?' says he, sitting up. 'What does she do ridiculous, I should like to know?' 'Why, wears a false front and curls bought at Frau Koelsch's shop,' says I. 'Poor thing, she can't make herself look young and beautiful, whatever she does, and Frau Rittmeister Bernstorf was laughing at her the other day, and at the high heels and at the stuffing the ***Schneiderin*** round the corner puts into her gowns to cover the angular bones! She would look much more respectable,' said I, 'if she would brush her scanty grey locks back, and smooth them with pomatum as I do, and wear a black lace ***Muetze*** over them, instead of making herself the laughing-stock of Schleswig.' And away I walked. And the Professor ate no supper that night, and next day he left for his ***Ferienausflug***, and never called to say good-bye to Fraeulein Meyer; and so I put the extinguisher on that little candle just as its flame was beginning to burn up, and-- why! here we are at Mainz."

And this is what I heard, and how I was entertained, in the "elektrische Bahn" on my little expedition from Wiesbaden to Mainz. I reflected, as I saw the Haushaelterin get down heavily with all the deliberation of her sixty-five and a half years, that feline amenities are much the same in Germany as in England; and I felt sorry for poor Fraeulein Meyer, who might have given up her small vanities and made pancakes and ***Apfelkuchen*** for the Professor quite as well in the end as the Haushaelterin.

The cathedral of Mainz was, of course, the object of our expedition. It dominates the city from afar, with its wonderful towers and pinnacles, making of Mainz (a commonplace city enough) a thing of beauty. From the shores of the Rhine we crossed a wide street planted with trees and lined on each hand with modern German houses of pinkish stone (covered with heavy sculpture and breaking out into countless balconies and bay windows), and soon found ourselves in the market-place. And here, indeed, one felt oneself in the Germany of bygone days. Instead of pseudo-classic buildings, heavy with meaningless ornamentation, we found beautiful old timber-framed houses, with deep eaves and wood carvings. On one of these I read:

Zum Kurfuerstlichen
Wappen.
Erneuert in Jahr
des Heils
1899.

It was evidently a Gasthaus of considerable antiquity, and had been carefully restored. Close by a Brobdingnagian finger lured the unwary to where it pointed--a low doorway above which was inscribed the legend: "Hier essen Sie gut." The market-place had been dismantled of its stalls and umbrellas all but one, which was being furled as we arrived on the scene. A couple of men in blue smocks were sweeping up the cabbage leaves, straw and refuse, market carts were driving off, and smart-looking officers in beautiful uniforms strolled across what we English miscall "a square" for want of a better word.

But to get a good view of the exterior of the cathedral was what we wanted, and to this end we dived down strange, evil-smelling alleys, and went round and round a labyrinth of streets, always expecting to see, and never arriving at, the cathedral's facade. At last we realised that the quest was hopeless, since the building is so surrounded and deformed by commonplace, ugly houses that nothing of it but roof and towers can be seen from outside. We entered it at last by a narrow lane between poor, ugly houses, an unfit approach indeed to this beautiful Romanesque cathedral--one of the four famous Romanesque Gothic cathedrals of Germany. The general effect of the interior is that of strength, solidity, and simplicity. The grand structural lines are noble and pure. There is an entire absence of the florid in architecture, and no attempt at all at decoration as one understands it in Spanish cathedrals. The tone of the walls and floor is a pinkish brown, and the whole church has a warm glowing effect from its richly-coloured stone. I could have spared most, if not all, of the overladen rococo monuments to the Electors of Mainz, with their monstrous records of impossible perfections; but my companion (a German lady) thought them beautiful. The whole church struck one as rather ill-kept; perhaps the red stone floor had something to do with it. Dust and mud do not adhere some-how to an opus Alexandrinum pavement. A guide appeared to offer his services, almost obsequiously polite in his attentions to the English lady. Whatever their opinions may be as to our failings and vices, our shortcomings and our iniquities, most Germans are civil to us nowadays.[3] They hate us cordially, envy us sincerely, attack us in the press and out of it, and are insanely jealous of the people they affect to despise. But while the superficial *entente* lasts, they smile and bow and are out-wardly polite. I asked an English lady, the widow of a German official, if her hus-band, having married an English wife, did not cherish kindlier sentiments towards us than the majority of his countrymen. "He died during the Boer war," she said, "and he died in the sure and certain hope that England was done for."

Apart from the Domkirche, there is little to see in Mainz, although the city is of great antiquity, having been founded by Drusus. It is a strongly fortified place, and stood once upon a time a memorable siege. There are pleasant walks by the Rhine, beautiful Anlagen, a picturesque old tower, and the site of Gutenberg's house to see. The Grand Ducal Palace once sheltered Napoleon the First, as did many another palace in Germany. The present Grand Duke prefers his palace in Darmstadt, the Neue Palais (built by Queen Victoria for Princess Alice), and comes little to the ancient city of bygone Electors.

We have fallen into German ways--alarming thought!--and become unques-tionably alive to the virtues of cafes and Restaurations as a wind-up to a day's ex-pedition. At Mainz we discovered a cafe close to the theatre, and sipped coffee and ate **Streuselkuchen** out of doors in the shadow of the cathedral and Gutenberg's statue. A pleasant-faced Gretchen brought us miniature Mont Blancs of whipped cream on small glass plates, and loitered near us ostensibly rearranging a table, but in reality studying our gowns and hats. Before we paid our Rechnung, the Haush-aelterin and Frau Rittergutsbesitzer turned up hot and rather cross, having spent their time since we parted in futile attempts to match Schleswig-Holstein ribbons with those of the sunny Rhineland.

---

3   This was written before the war.

SCHLANGENBAD.
GREEN HILLS AND BLUE WATERS.

Schlangenbad, although a charmingly pretty spot, is not one to fascinate a painter. The landscape is unvaryingly green, and that green is too monotonous in tone for effect in a picture. Moreover, it lies shut in by hills, and there is no distant horizon to give the value of foreground and middle distance. But less critical eyes find much to admire in Schlangenbad. The great wide road leading to it from Eltville testifies to its former popularity in the days of family coaches and postilions. Nowadays an ugly steam tram transports the traveller from the Rhine to the "Serpent's Bath," and nearly poisons and chokes him *en route* with the horrible smoke it emits. Half of the tram is open to the air at the sides, like a char-a-banc; and when we travelled by it a little party of Germans were enjoying an *Ausflug*, each man with one eye cocked on the scenery and the other on the look-out for a *Bier-garten*.

Next to me sat a student, whose face was so slashed and gashed that it reminded one of "Amtshauptmann Weber" (in Reuter's delightful book), whose "face looked as if he had sat down upon it on a cane-bottomed chair." Opposite the student was a middle-aged fat "Assessor," with a small girl in long frilled drawers and short petticoats; and on the other side of the gangway were two homely-looking women in lead-coloured garments. As we passed through Altdorf the child drew her father's attention to a fat goose which waddled away as the tram approached. "Sieh mal, Vater," said she, "die schoene Gans." ("Look, father, at the beautiful goose.") "O! *die Gans*," said her practical and prosaic parent, "wird viel schoener sein, mein Kind, wenn sie gebraten ist." ("The goose will be much more beautiful, my child, when it is roast.") "And has an accompaniment of sage-stuffing and apple-sauce," I added, to which he in all serious conviction bowed an assent.

The valley up which we journeyed was green and pleasant. There were no walls or fences on either side of the road, but trees shaded the wayfarer, and his out-look on gardens, bean-poles, orchards, and vines was agreeable enough. If he chose to look further afield a silvery streak called the Rhine was visible, and beyond that again low blue hills stretched away until their cobalt and that of the sky got mixed on the palette of Nature. From this valley comes the famous Rauen-thaler wine. Most of the hills, indeed, are covered with vines, and the village houses showed grapes hanging from their eaves and peeping in at their windows.

At Neudorf we paused to pick up a ***Barmherzige Schwester***; and as our halt was exactly in front of the village shop I amused myself by making a mental inventory of its contents. The window--an ordinary one--had wooden shelves nailed across it; and on these were displayed soap, slates and slate-pencils, bottles of peppermint lozenges, hearthstone, flannel, lemon-drops, gingham, sausages, and gingerbread.

The houses of the village were covered with rough stucco, and white or yellow-wash was swished liberally over them. Under their deep eaves an occasional small image of ***Die Mutter Gottes*** was to be seen. Many were covered with grape-vines, and all had clean muslin blinds at their windows, and often pots of geraniums and fuchsias outside. Sunflowers, dahlias, and roses grew in the little patches of garden by the road; and all was charming and primitive, save for the discordant electric fittings which hung midway on the telegraph-posts, and the anomaly of a brand new brick ***Brod-fabrik*** just outside the village.

All the way up the "cane-bottomed chair" and the "Assessor" smoked stolidly, while their women-folk cackled like human geese. "Wie schoen!" "Colossal!" "En-tzueckend!" "Reizend!" Nothing but incessant and weary adjectives! I turned with relief to the "Barmherzige Schwester," a prim and silent little figure in neat blue cotton gown, black apron, and white kerchief pinned over her shining hair.

The tram stopped at last before the village church, and we all got out. To our left, as we faced the Kurhaus, straggled a long line of houses with deep verandahs and balconies, to our right shady walks and bath-houses and beautiful woods. Here and there amid the hotels and villas was a shop, and we knew that Schlangenbad marched with the times when we saw the word "Schamponieren" and a bunch of Empire curls exhibited as a modern trophy. We stopped at a shop and examined its wares, which, indeed, hung chiefly on the shutters. There were Swiss embroidered gowns and blouses to be bought, edelweiss penwipers, wooden paper-cutters, and clocks with chamois climbing wooden rocks. Nothing apparently in that shop had been "made in Germany." When we reached the verandah of the "Nassauer Hof" we were gladdened by bows from the "Assessor" and the student, who with the "cackling geese" were seated at a long table consuming piles of Apfelkuchen, Streuselkuchen, and Napfkuchen to an accompaniment of steaming coffee.

As for dull, useful information Schlangenbad, of course, was known to the Romans, and they bathed in its waters. The Middle Ages seem to have neglected Spas generally, and to have been dead to the joys of a bath. At all events, nothing more was heard about Schlangenbad or its springs until in 1687 a wooden hut was put over what was known as the "Roemer Bad." Next the Landgraf of Hesse awoke to the virtues of its waters, and caused the "Oberes Kurhaus" to be built. Five years later, the "Nassauer Hof" was erected, and a time of prosperity and fashion set in for Schlangenbad. The waters have always had a great reputation for beautifying the skin and healing wounds and sores. It is on record that Frederick the First of Sweden ordered four thousand bottles of Schlangenbad water a year as ***eau de toilette***, and another and still vainer sovereign three hundred a week. After this who shall dare say that women have the monopoly of vanity?

Besides embellishing, the Schlangenbad waters are good in nervous disorders, rheumatism, and asthma. They are of an exquisite light-blue colour, and when bathing in them one's limbs have the appearance of marble. That the Schlangenbad people think highly of their "cure" is obvious. I bought a map of the district (manufactured in the place) and found the word Schlangenbad printed in huge letters, while the neighbouring town of Wiesbaden was in such small ones that it looked as if scarcely worth mentioning at all.

LIEBENSTEIN.

Here in the Thuringian Forest, aloof from the stir and roar of life, lies a Kur-Ort little known to the English world. Its waters are analogous to those of Schwalbach, its air is as pure, its scenery more beautiful, and its prices half those of the Taunus Wald. Its people still retain their primitive charm, unspoilt as yet by the potentialities of South African or American money-bags. Within easy reach of such interesting towns as Eisenach, Weimar, Erfurt, Gotha, and Coburg, it offers many alluring baits to the sightseer; yet to the coming and going of tourists is it altogether unaccustomed. Liebenstein lies in a green and beautiful valley, and the hills which surround it are covered for the most part with great black forests. Patches of wheat and rye vibrate in the winds which sweep up the valleys, and the fields of potatoes alternate on the low grounds with pasturage and orchards. Under the great limestone rocks, which near Liebenstein rise sheer out of the plain, nestle charming villages, and long avenues of poplars conduct you where you would go along the high roads. By the roadside a wealth of flowers is yours for the picking--wild thyme and asparagus and mallow, periwinkles, and the picturesque dock and crowfoot. The woods are starred with flowers, and the perfume of the pines is a revelation.

The humbler houses of Liebenstein (for the greater part timber-framed and red-tiled) straggle up the immediate hills which surround it. Those of more pretention and inevitable ugliness range themselves decently and in order along two parallel roads. Aloof as this village is from "the madding crowd's ignoble strife," it has yet been touched to its undoing by the ruthless finger of conventionality. The inevitable Kur-Haus and bandstand and Anlagen are here; worst of all, a Trink-Halle! The Trink-Halle stands a mute and awful warning to the vaulting ambition which overleaps itself, since a classic temple in the heart of Liebenstein is surely as much out of place as a tiara would be on the head of the peasant woman who hands you your daily portion of Stahlwasser. Even the spring it originally sheltered has revolted against its sham marble pillars and grotesque entablature, and betaken itself elsewhere! Nowadays the paint and plaster are peeling off the columns, and its door is padlocked. Happily--although a melancholy warning to the educated--it remains a source of pride to the peasant, who loves his shabby temple as the Romans do the marble glories of their Vesta.

Immediately behind the temple are the springs of Georg and Kasimir, at which stand two charming maidens ready to fill your glasses. No conventional and hideous hat or bonnet disfigures the neat outline of their heads. No travesty of Berlin or Paris fashion burlesques their sturdy figures. Theirs the traditional costume of the Thuringian female peasant--a dark skirt, and white, short-sleeved chemisette, a blue apron and the daintiest of white silk kerchiefs, fringed sparsely and brocaded abundantly with red roses. Albeit their arms are red and coarse with the combined effect of iron-water, hot sun, and exposure to the air, their faces make ample amends in their innocent, good-tempered comeliness. They greet you with a kindly "Guten Tag" or "Guten Abend," and, in the case of a lady, seldom omit the pretty "Gnaedige Frau," for which our "Ma'am" is but a poor correlative.

Wandering through the streets of Liebenstein, one is struck by the intensely picturesque sights of its older and original part. The little houses are timber-framed and whitewashed, with deep projecting eaves and often many gables. Their windows are made gay outside by boxes filled with geraniums, nasturtiums, and fuchsias. Beneath the windows lie small gardens, in which bloom roses and single dahlias, while scarlet runners send their tendrils climbing over the palings which separate road and garden. Many of the little houses have projecting signs, on which one reads such legends as "Tabak, Cigarren, Cigaretten;" "Adolf Schmidt, **Herren kleidermacher**;" "Weinhandlung Naturreinheit garantirt;" or the very indispensable "Baeckerei." One house bears a tablet announcing to an admiring world that "Herzoglich. Sachsen-Meiningen Stadtesbeamter" lives within. Cocks and hens, dogs and children, make common playground of these narrow streets, and one sees in them pretty well every form of animal life represented, except horses. Now a long cart, drawn by oxen and well filled, toils up the hill, and not long after follows one drawn by a big dog. At a pump two tiny girls are busily employed filling stone jars, which by the beauty and purity of their outlines might have been Etruscan. Mothers beat mats at their cottage doors, and shrilly scream at their children to get out of the way of the passing carts; and the world in this remote village goes on pretty much as it does elsewhere.

But the fashionable life of Liebenstein does not concern itself with such mean sights and bucolic sounds as oxen-carts and crowing of cocks. It takes its pleasure up and down the long avenues of beech trees which lie between the Kur-Haus and the Hotel Bellevue. It rallies round the bandstand, and makes great show of studying the programmes of the daily concert. It chatters glibly over the previous evening's illuminations, and describes them as "colossal!" and "wunderschoen." Beauty is not in vogue at Liebenstein, judging by the middle-class Kur guests who haunt the shade of the beech trees. Indeed, if anywhere in the world an Englishman might be forgiven for thanking God that he is not as other men are, it would be here among the "Ober-Lieutenants" and "Herr Professors" and their mates. Figures, both male and female, seem to be of the switchback order--faces rudimentary in their model-ling, and uncompromising in their plainness, dressing of the ugliest. Yet, **Gott sei Dank!** Hans thinks his Gretchen perfection, and it would never enter into innocent Gretchen's head, as it does mine, to bestow upon Hans the carping criticism of Portia upon Monsieur Le Bon: "God made him, and therefore let him pass for a man."

TREVES

The dominant glory of the Moselle region is Treves. No town or city near has the smallest affinity with its peculiar character, and all seem modern and prosaic compared with its well-preserved tale of antiquity. "Nowhere north of the Alps," we are told in weary iteration, "exist such magnificent Roman remains." It is generally on the obvious that the unimaginative English parson takes upon himself to comment. We listen submissively to much school-book lore as to "Claudius" and the "fourth century" and the "residence of Roman Emperors," but when it rains Bishops and Archbishops and Electors we fly before them. For, after all, what signifies the paltry learning of a dry-as-dust dominie compared with the vivid tales these grand old ruins tell if suffered to speak for themselves? In Treves people need to absorb silently, and then assimilate undisturbed by weary chatter. One looks at the tender turquoise sky, flecked with luminous clouds; at the fine horizontal distance, with its sense of breadth and breathing-space; at the low hills covered with vines; at the cornfields, and orchards, and river--and we wonder what the old Romans thought of it all, and reflect on the strangeness of life that a people so remote from our times should have lived and loved and died, as we live and love and die to-day. Whether Treves lie on the right or left bank of the Moselle is immaterial except to the tiresomely precise or to those who pin their faith to guide-books and such shallow teachers. There is a more valuable lesson to be learnt of the place than that of its exact situation; and no Baedeker or Murray can help you to appreciate Treves as quiet communings with your own intelligence will. If it so happens that you have none to commune with, then God help you--and yours!

In Treves you have not far to go in search of the Romans. Their *magnum opus* confronts you boldly at the very threshold of the town. Solid and massive and symmetrical, it stands a pregnant lesson to the jerry-builders of to-day. There is little affinity indeed between the building methods of the ancient Romans and those of their trade whose sorry, pitiable record exists in the Quartiere Nuovo of Rome. About the Porta Nigra is no trace of stucco or rubble. The huge blocks of which it is built stand one upon the other clean-hewn and square. No signs of mortar are left, but we see marks of iron or brass clamps. Its colour is a warm, deep red, softened here and there by streaks of green.

The Porta Nigra has passed through strange phases since first it started in life as a city gate. Obviously built for purposes of fortification, and equipped with towers of defence, its second phase was an ecclesiastical one, and the "spears" were indeed turned into "pruning-hooks" when the bellicose propugnaculum found itself transformed into a church.

> "Last scene of all,
> That ends this strange, eventful history."

The gate was in 1876 finally cleared of priests and altars, and allowed to revert to its original form.

Not far from the Porta Nigra stands the Cathedral, one of the oldest in Germany, archaeologically interesting, inasmuch as it owes its inception to the Romans. The Basilica, built by Valentinian as a court of law, is clearly traceable in the present cathedral, and one reads a strange tale of Romans and Franks in the sandstone and limestone and brick of its walls. Here is treasured the famous Heilige Rock, or holy coat worn by our Saviour when a boy. At rare intervals this garment is exhibited to the faithful, who come from all countries to gaze reverently upon it. Who that has seen can forget the last exposition in 1891? Never before or since has there been anything more pathetic than the sight of the long rows of tired, haggard, perspiring, praying pilgrims, who stood patiently for hours in the broiling August sun, moving only when permitted, and then at a snail's pace, towards their Mecca. Plebeian though the majority of faces were, their devotional, solemn, rapt expressions for the time being ennobled and beautified them.

Treves during that time, however, was by no means the reposeful, dignified city it is to-day. Its buildings were defaced with flags and banners, its streets blocked with pilgrims, and the road leading from the station to the town was lined with booths, whose owners disposed quickly of such delicacies as Napfkuchen, Streusel-Kuchen, and Apfelwein. Piety and profit went everywhere hand-in-hand, and a roaring trade was done in rosaries and benitiers, the last made of the blue pottery of the country, and stamped with a representation of Leo XIII. against a background of Domkirche.

But to be thoroughly in harmony with Treves one must be Pagan and Roman rather than Christian and German. Indeed, one feels in sympathy with the Isle of Wight farmer who after he had found a Roman villa on his farm gave up the bucolic and inglorious occupation of growing turnips and potatoes, and could talk of nothing meaner than hypocausts and thermae. So we, like the farmer, slight the really beautiful Early Gothic "Liebfrauenkirche" and roam and muse for hours about the ruins of the Amphitheatre, the Roman Baths, the Roman Palace and the Basilica.

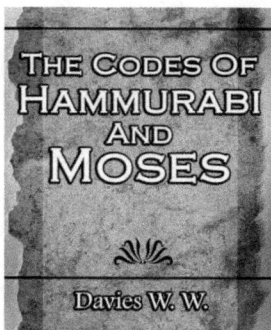

The Codes Of Hammurabi And Moses
W. W. Davies

QTY

The discovery of the Hammurabi Code is one of the greatest achievements of archaeology, and is of paramount interest, not only to the student of the Bible, but also to all those interested in ancient history...

Religion   **ISBN:** *1-59462-338-4*   **Pages:132**
MSRP $12.95

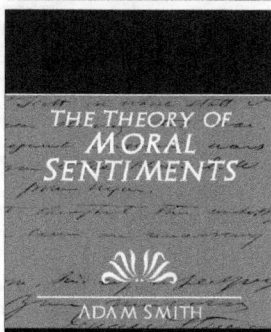

The Theory of Moral Sentiments
Adam Smith

QTY

This work from 1749. contains original theories of conscience amd moral judgment and it is the foundation for systemof morals.

Philosophy   **ISBN:** *1-59462-777-0*   **Pages:536**
MSRP $19.95

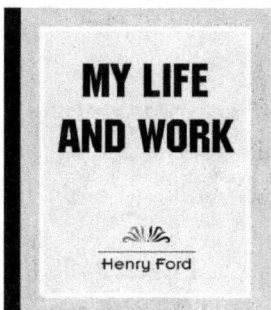

Jessica's First Prayer
Hesba Stretton

QTY

In a screened and secluded corner of one of the many railway-bridges which span the streets of London there could be seen a few years ago, from five o'clock every morning until half past eight, a tidily set-out coffee-stall, consisting of a trestle and board, upon which stood two large tin cans, with a small fire of charcoal burning under each so as to keep the coffee boiling during the early hours of the morning when the work-people were thronging into the city on their way to their daily toil...

Pages:84

Childrens   **ISBN:** *1-59462-373-2*   *MSRP $9.95*

My Life and Work
Henry Ford

QTY

Henry Ford revolutionized the world with his implementation of mass production for the Model T automobile. Gain valuable business insight into his life and work with his own auto-biography... "We have only started on our development of our country we have not as yet, with all our talk of wonderful progress, done more than scratch the surface. The progress has been wonderful enough but..."

Pages:300

Biographies/   **ISBN:** *1-59462-198-5*   *MSRP $21.95*

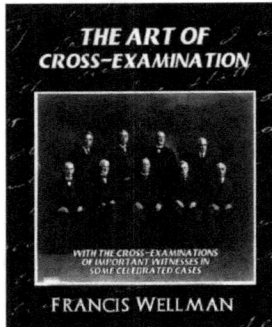

The Art of Cross-Examination
Francis Wellman

QTY

I presume it is the experience of every author, after his first book is published upon an important subject, to be almost overwhelmed with a wealth of ideas and illustrations which could readily have been included in his book, and which to his own mind, at least, seem to make a second edition inevitable. Such certainly was the case with me; and when the first edition had reached its sixth impression in five months, I rejoiced to learn that it seemed to my publishers that the book had met with a sufficiently favorable reception to justify a second and considerably enlarged edition. ..

Reference   ISBN: *1-59462-647-2*

Pages:412

MSRP $19.95

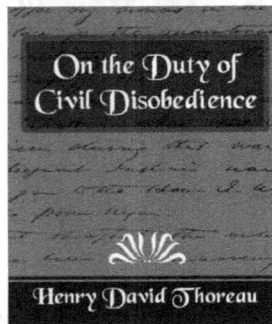

On the Duty of Civil Disobedience
Henry David Thoreau

QTY

Thoreau wrote his famous essay, On the Duty of Civil Disobedience, as a protest against an unjust but popular war and the immoral but popular institution of slave-owning. He did more than write—he declined to pay his taxes, and was hauled off to gaol in consequence. Who can say how much this refusal of his hastened the end of the war and of slavery ?

Law   ISBN: *1-59462-747-9*

Pages:48

MSRP $7.45

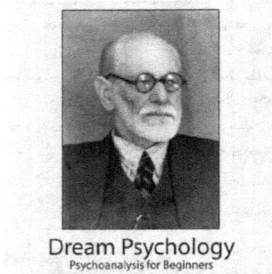

Dream Psychology Psychoanalysis for Beginners
Sigmund Freud

QTY

Sigmund Freud, born Sigismund Schlomo Freud (May 6, 1856 - September 23, 1939), was a Jewish-Austrian neurologist and psychiatrist who co-founded the psychoanalytic school of psychology. Freud is best known for his theories of the unconscious mind, especially involving the mechanism of repression; his redefinition of sexual desire as mobile and directed towards a wide variety of objects; and his therapeutic techniques, especially his understanding of transference in the therapeutic relationship and the presumed value of dreams as sources of insight into unconscious desires.

Psychology   ISBN: *1-59462-905-6*

Pages:196

MSRP $15.45

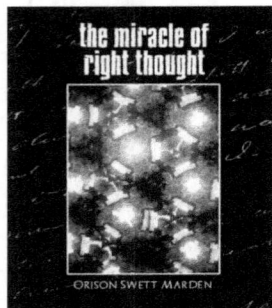

The Miracle of Right Thought
Orison Swett Marden

QTY

Believe with all of your heart that you will do what you were made to do. When the mind has once formed the habit of holding cheerful, happy, prosperous pictures, it will not be easy to form the opposite habit. It does not matter how improbable or how far away this realization may see, or how dark the prospects may be, if we visualize them as best we can, as vividly as possible, hold tenaciously to them and vigorously struggle to attain them, they will gradually become actualized, realized in the life. But a desire, a longing without endeavor, a yearning abandoned or held indifferently will vanish without realization.

Self Help   ISBN: *1-59462-644-8*

Pages:360

MSRP $25.45

www.bookjungle.com *email: sales@bookjungle.com fax: 630-214-0564 mail: Book Jungle PO Box 2226 Champaign, IL 61825*

QTY

The Rosicrucian Cosmo-Conception Mystic Christianity by *Max Heindel*   ISBN: *1-59462-188-8*   **$38.95**
The Rosicrucian Cosmo-conception is not dogmatic, neither does it appeal to any other authority than the reason of the student. It is: not controversial, but is: sent forth in the, hope that it may help to clear...   New Age/Religion Pages 646

Abandonment To Divine Providence by *Jean-Pierre de Caussade*   ISBN: *1-59462-228-0*   **$25.95**
"The Rev. Jean Pierre de Caussade was one of the most remarkable spiritual writers of the Society of Jesus in France in the 18th Century. His death took place at Toulouse in 1751. His works have gone through many editions and have been republished...   Inspirational/Religion Pages 400

Mental Chemistry by *Charles Haanel*   ISBN: *1-59462-192-6*   **$23.95**
Mental Chemistry allows the change of material conditions by combining and appropriately utilizing the power of the mind. Much like applied chemistry creates something new and unique out of careful combinations of chemicals the mastery of mental chemistry...   New Age/Business Pages 354

The Letters of Robert Browning and Elizabeth Barret Barrett 1845-1846 vol II   ISBN: *1-59462-193-4*   **$35.95**
by *Robert Browning* and *Elizabeth Barrett*   Biographies Pages 596

Gleanings In Genesis (volume I) by *Arthur W. Pink*   ISBN: *1-59462-130-6*   **$27.45**
Appropriately has Genesis been termed "the seed plot of the Bible" for in it we have, in germ form, almost all of the great doctrines which are afterwards fully developed in the books of Scripture which follow...   Religion/Inspirational Pages 420

The Master Key by *L. W. de Laurence*   ISBN: *1-59462-001-6*   **$30.95**
In no branch of human knowledge has there been a more lively increase of the spirit of research during the past few years than in the study of Psychology, Concentration and Mental Discipline. The requests for authentic lessons in Thought Control, Mental Discipline and...   New Age/Occult Pages 422

The Lesser Key Of Solomon Goetia by *L. W. de Laurence*   ISBN: *1-59462-092-X*   **$9.95**
This translation of the first book of the "Lernegton" which is now for the first time made accessible to students of Talismanic Magic was done, after careful collation and edition, from numerous Ancient Manuscripts in Hebrew, Latin, and French...   New Age/Occult Pages 92

Rubaiyat Of Omar Khayyam by *Edward Fitzgerald*   ISBN:*1-59462-332-5*   **$13.95**
Edward Fitzgerald, whom the world has already learned, in spite of his own efforts to remain within the shadow of anonymity, to look upon as one of the rarest poets of the century, was born at Bredfield, in Suffolk, on the 31st of March, 1809. He was the third son of John Purcell...   Music Pages 172

Ancient Law by *Henry Maine*   ISBN: *1-59462-128-4*   **$29.95**
The chief object of the following pages is to indicate some of the earliest ideas of mankind, as they are reflected in Ancient Law, and to point out the relation of those ideas to modern thought.   Religion/History Pages 452

Far-Away Stories by *William J. Locke*   ISBN: *1-59462-129-2*   **$19.45**
"Good wine needs no bush, but a collection of mixed vintages does. And this book is just such a collection. Some of the stories I do not want to remain buried for ever in the museum files of dead magazine-numbers an author's not unpardonable vanity..."   Fiction Pages 272

Life of David Crockett by *David Crockett*   ISBN: *1-59462-250-7*   **$27.45**
"Colonel David Crockett was one of the most remarkable men of the times in which he lived. Born in humble life, but gifted with a strong will, an indomitable courage, and unremitting perseverance...   Biographies/New Age Pages 424

Lip-Reading by *Edward Nitchie*   ISBN: *1-59462-206-X*   **$25.95**
Edward B. Nitchie, founder of the New York School for the Hard of Hearing, now the Nitchie School of Lip-Reading, Inc, wrote "LIP-READING Principles and Practice". The development and perfecting of this meritorious work on lip-reading was an undertaking...   How-to Pages 400

A Handbook of Suggestive Therapeutics, Applied Hypnotism, Psychic Science   ISBN: *1-59462-214-0*   **$24.95**
by *Henry Munro*   Health/New Age/Health/Self-help Pages 376

A Doll's House: and Two Other Plays by *Henrik Ibsen*   ISBN: *1-59462-112-8*   **$19.95**
Henrik Ibsen created this classic when in revolutionary 1848 Rome. Introducing some striking concepts in playwriting for the realist genre, this play has been studied the world over.   Fiction/Classics/Plays 308

The Light of Asia by *sir Edwin Arnold*   ISBN: *1-59462-204-3*   **$13.95**
In this poetic masterpiece, Edwin Arnold describes the life and teachings of Buddha. The man who was to become known as Buddha to the world was born as Prince Gautama of India but he rejected the worldly riches and abandoned the reigns of power when...   Religion/History/Biographies Pages 170

The Complete Works of Guy de Maupassant by *Guy de Maupassant*   ISBN: *1-59462-157-8*   **$16.95**
"For days and days, nights and nights, I had dreamed of that first kiss which was to consecrate our engagement, and I knew not on what spot I should put my lips..."   Fiction/Classics Pages 240

The Art of Cross-Examination by *Francis L. Wellman*   ISBN: *1-59462-309-0*   **$26.95**
Written by a renowned trial lawyer, Wellman imparts his experience and uses case studies to explain how to use psychology to extract desired information through questioning.   How-to/Science/Reference Pages 408

Answered or Unanswered? by *Louisa Vaughan*   ISBN: *1-59462-248-5*   **$10.95**
Miracles of Faith in China   Religion Pages 112

The Edinburgh Lectures on Mental Science (1909) by *Thomas*   ISBN: *1-59462-008-3*   **$11.95**
This book contains the substance of a course of lectures recently given by the writer in the Queen Street Hall, Edinburgh. Its purpose is to indicate the Natural Principles governing the relation between Mental Action and Material Conditions...   New Age/Psychology Pages 148

Ayesha by *H. Rider Haggard*   ISBN: *1-59462-301-5*   **$24.95**
Verily and indeed it is the unexpected that happens! Probably if there was one person upon the earth from whom the Editor of this, and of a certain previous history, did not expect to hear again...   Classics Pages 380

Ayala's Angel by *Anthony Trollope*   ISBN: *1-59462-352-X*   **$29.95**
The two girls were both pretty, but Lucy who was twenty-one who supposed to be simple and comparatively unattractive, whereas Ayala was credited, as her Bombwhat romantic name might show, with poetic charm and a taste for romance. Ayala when her father died was nineteen...   Fiction Pages 484

The American Commonwealth by *James Bryce*   ISBN: *1-59462-286-8*   **$34.45**
An interpretation of American democratic political theory. It examines political mechanics and society from the perspective of Scotsman James Bryce   Politics Pages 572

Stories of the Pilgrims by *Margaret P. Pumphrey*   ISBN: *1-59462-116-0*   **$17.95**
This book explores pilgrims religious oppression in England as well as their escape to Holland and eventual crossing to America on the Mayflower, and their early days in New England...   History Pages 268

QTY

The Fasting Cure *by Sinclair Upton*   ISBN: *1-59462-222-1* **$13.95**
In the Cosmopolitan Magazine for May, 1910, and in the Contemporary Review (London) for April, 1910, I published an article dealing with my experiences in fasting. I have written a great many magazine articles, but never one which attracted so much attention... New Age/Self Help/Health Pages 164

Hebrew Astrology *by Sepharial*   ISBN: *1-59462-308-2* **$13.45**
In these days of advanced thinking it is a matter of common observation that we have left many of the old landmarks behind and that we are now pressing forward to greater heights and to a wider horizon than that which represented the mind-content of our progenitors... Astrology Pages 144

Thought Vibration or The Law of Attraction in the Thought World   ISBN: *1-59462-127-6* **$12.95**
by William Walker Atkinson   *Psychology/Religion Pages 144*

Optimism *by Helen Keller*   ISBN: *1-59462-108-X* **$15.95**
Helen Keller was blind, deaf, and mute since 19 months old, yet famously learned how to overcome these handicaps, communicate with the world, and spread her lectures promoting optimism. An inspiring read for everyone... Biographies/Inspirational Pages 84

Sara Crewe *by Frances Burnett*   ISBN: *1-59462-360-0* **$9.45**
In the first place, Miss Minchin lived in London. Her home was a large, dull, tall one, in a large, dull square, where all the houses were alike, and all the sparrows were alike, and where all the door-knockers made the same heavy sound... Childrens/Classic Pages 88

The Autobiography of Benjamin Franklin *by Benjamin Franklin*   ISBN: *1-59462-135-7* **$24.95**
The Autobiography of Benjamin Franklin has probably been more extensively read than any other American historical work, and no other book of its kind has had such ups and downs of fortune. Franklin lived for many years in England, where he was agent... Biographies/History Pages 332

Name	
Email	
Telephone	
Address	
City, State ZIP	

☐ **Credit Card**   ☐ **Check / Money Order**

Credit Card Number	
Expiration Date	
Signature	

Please Mail to: Book Jungle
PO Box 2226
Champaign, IL 61825
or Fax to: 630-214-0564

ORDERING INFORMATION
web*: www.bookjungle.com*
email*: sales@bookjungle.com*
fax*: 630-214-0564*
mail*: Book Jungle PO Box 2226 Champaign, IL 61825*
or PayPal *to sales@bookjungle.com*

Please contact us for bulk discounts

DIRECT-ORDER TERMS

**20% Discount if You Order
Two or More Books**
Free Domestic Shipping!
Accepted: Master Card, Visa,
Discover, American Express

www.ingramcontent.com/pod-product-compliance
Lightning Source LLC
LaVergne TN
LVHW081326060426
835511LV00011B/1883